PROTEIN
on MyPlate

by Mari Schuh

Consulting editor: Gail Saunders-Smith, PhD

Consultant: Barbara J. Rolls, PhD
Guthrie Chair in Nutrition
Pennsylvania State University
University Park, Pennsylvania

CAPSTONE PRESS
a capstone imprint

Pebble Plus is published by Capstone Press,
1710 Roe Crest Drive, North Mankato, Minnesota 56003.
www.capstonepub.com

The author dedicates this book to Devon Borst of Pleasant Prairie, Wisconsin,
who makes the best hard-boiled eggs in southeastern Wisconsin.

Library of Congress Cataloging-in-Publication Data
Schuh, Mari C., 1975–
 Protein on myplate / by Mari Schuh.
   p. cm.—(Pebble plus. What's on myplate?)
 Includes bibliographical references and index.
 Summary: "Simple text and photos describe USDA's MyPlate tool and healthy protein choices
for children"—Provided by publisher.
 ISBN 978-1-4296-8745-4 (library binding)
 ISBN 978-1-4296-9420-9 (paperback)
 ISBN 978-1-620655- (eBook PDF)
 1. Proteins in human nutrition—Juvenile literature. I. Title.
TX553.P7S38 2013
612'.01575—dc23   2012009315

Information in this book supports
the U.S. Department of Agriculture's
MyPlate food guidance system found at
www.choosemyplate.gov. Food amounts
listed in this book are based on daily
recommendations for children ages 4-8.
The amounts listed in this book are
appropriate for children who get less than
30 minutes a day of moderate physical
activity, beyond normal daily activities.
Children who are more physically active
may be able to eat more while staying
within calorie needs. The U.S. Department
of Agriculture (USDA) does not endorse
any products, services, or organizations.

Editorial Credits
Jeni Wittrock, editor; Sarah Bennett, designer; Svetlana Zhurkin, media researcher; Kathy McColley,
   production specialist; Sarah Schuette, photo stylist; Marcy Morin, studio scheduler

Photo Credits
All photos by Capstone Studio/Karon Dubke except:
Shutterstock: BW Folsom, cover (bottom left), Igor Klimov, cover (top right), Pshenichka, cover (bottom right), Tristan
Tan, back cover; USDA, cover (inset), 5

Note to Parents and Teachers

The What's on MyPlate? series supports national science standards related to health and
nutrition. This book describes and illustrates the USDA's recommendations on protein. The
images support early readers in understanding the text. The repetition of words and phrases
helps early readers learn new words. This book also introduces early readers to subject-specific
vocabulary words, which are defined in the Glossary section. Early readers may need assistance
to read some words and to use the Table of Contents, Glossary, Read More, Internet Sites, and
Index sections of the book.

Printed in the United States of America in North Mankato, Minnesota.
042012   006682CGF12

Table of Contents

MyPlate

Protein foods are

an important part of MyPlate.

MyPlate is a tool that helps

you choose healthful food.

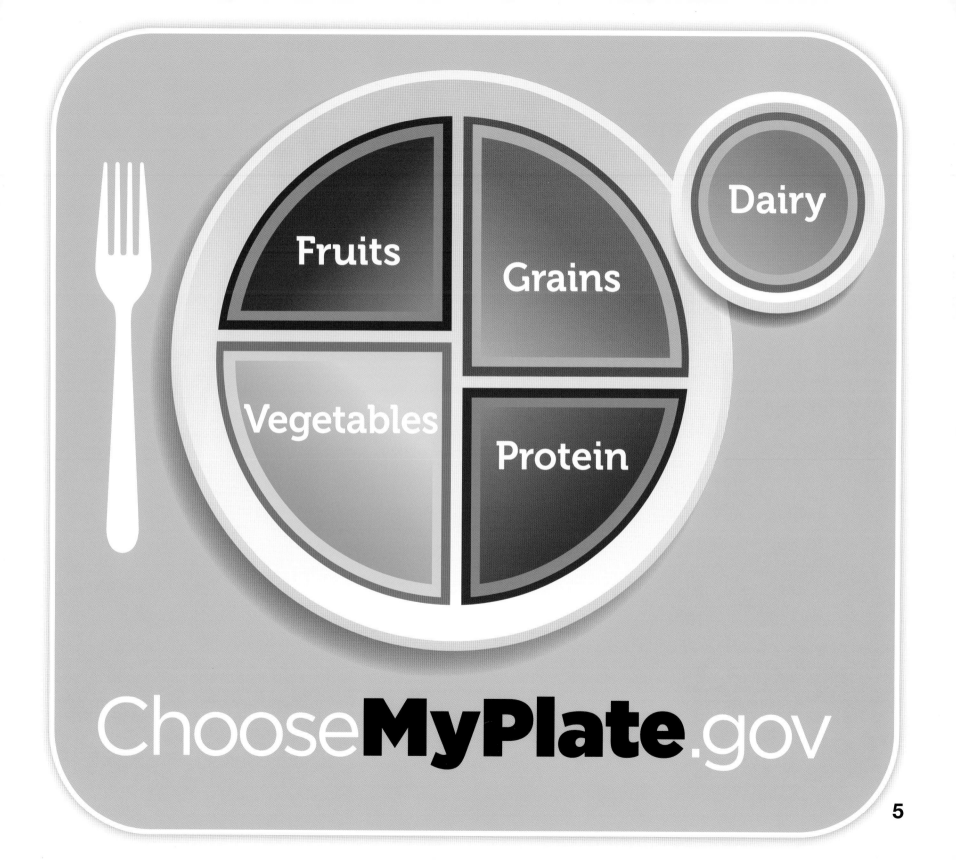

ChooseMyPlate.gov

5

Protein

Meats like chicken, beef, and fish are protein foods.

Beans, eggs, nuts, and seeds are also full of protein.

Protein helps build
bones and muscles.
Protein-rich foods
are full of nutrients.

Every day, eat 4 ounces
(110 grams) of protein.
Try to eat different
protein foods every week.

Eat lean protein.

Lean protein is low in fat.

Have an adult trim away

the fat from meat

before cooking.

Enjoying Protein Foods

Good morning!

Start the day with protein.

Eat ham and eggs

for breakfast.

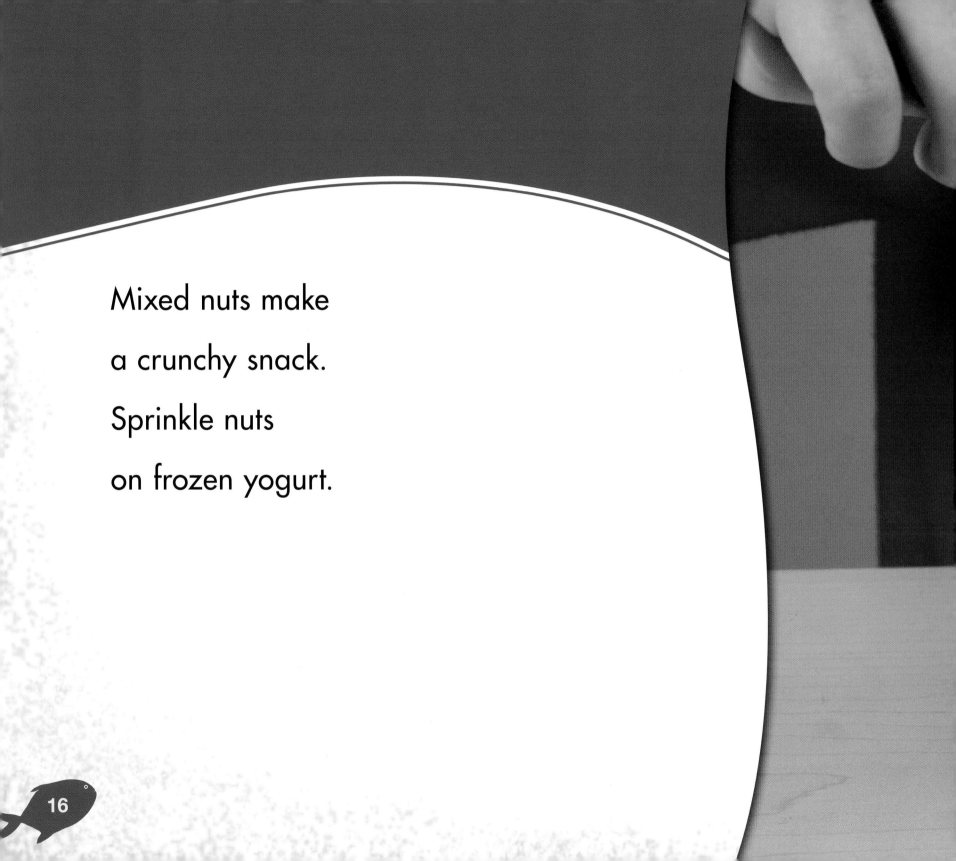

Mixed nuts make
a crunchy snack.
Sprinkle nuts
on frozen yogurt.

It's lunchtime.

Make a sandwich.

Choose peanut butter,

tuna, sliced lean meat,

or a veggie burger.

On a cold night,

warm up with chili

made with meat and beans.

What protein foods

will you choose tomorrow?

21

How Much to Eat

Many kids need to eat about 4 ounces (110 grams) of protein every day. To get 4 ounces, pick four servings of your favorite foods below.

¼ cup (60 mL) refried beans

½ ounce (15 grams) sunflower seeds

2 tablespoons (30 mL) hummus

½ veggie burger

1 tablespoon (15 mL) peanut butter

1 egg

1 ounce (30 grams) tuna

1 slice lean turkey

Glossary

MyPlate—a food plan that reminds people to eat healthful food and be active; MyPlate was created by the U.S. Department of Agriculture

muscle—a tissue in the body that is made of strong fibers; muscles can be tightened or relaxed to make the body move

nutrient—something that people need to eat to stay healthy and strong; vitamins and minerals are nutrients

protein—a substance found in plant and animal cells; your body needs protein to stay healthy

veggie burger—a burger made from vegetables, soybeans, and nuts; veggie burgers do not have any meat in them

Read More

Adams, Julia. *Proteins.* Good Food. New York: PowerKids Press, 2011.

Borgert-Spaniol, Megan. *Protein Foods Group.* Eating Right with MyPlate. Minneapolis: Bellwether Media, 2012.

Lee, Sally. *The Powerful Protein Group.* MyPlate and Healthy Eating. Mankato, Minn.: Capstone Press, 2012.

Internet Sites

FactHound offers a safe, fun way to find Internet sites related to this book. All of the sites on FactHound have been researched by our staff.

Here's all you do:

Visit *www.facthound.com*

Type in this code: 9781429687454

 Check out projects, games and lots more at www.capstonekids.com

Index

bones, 8

breakfast, 14

fat, 12

lean proteins, 12

lunch, 18

muscles, 8

MyPlate, 4

nutrients, 8

servings, 10, 22

snacks, 16

Word Count: 146
Grade: 1
Early-Intervention Level: 15